Go ahead, BE SO EMOTIONAL

Empowering *the* Emotional Personality To *do* Awesome Exploits *for* God

BEN R. PETERS

GO AHEAD, BE SO EMOTIONAL
© 2003 by Ben R. Peters

ISBN: 0-9767685-6-9

Unless otherwise indicated, Bible quotations are taken from the New King James Version. Copyright © 1983 by Thomas Nelson, Inc.

Cover art used by permission of Robert Bartow
www.bartowimages.com

Open Heart Ministries
15648 Bombay Blvd.
S. Beloit, IL 61080
www.ohmint.org
benrpeters@juno.com

Contents

Preface

This book is for two different groups of people: Those who have been accused of being too emotional and those who haven't. If you haven't, perhaps you are one that has accused others of being too emotional. For you, we trust that what you read in this small book will give you more understanding and appreciation for those you may have looked down on in some way in the past.

God made us all with a unique combination of talents, gifts, and personality traits. Our genetics and environmental factors interact with each other in many complex ways. No single categorization, such as motivational gifts, the four main personality types, left-brained/right-brained, male/female, etc., can perfectly identify who we are.

Obviously, we all have emotions, and we all have some level of intelligence. Some people think and carefully prepare before they speak or write a word. Others speak more spontaneously from the heart and emotions. Some may have very strong emotions, but manage to hold their emotions within themselves.

Although I have taken several university and seminary courses on Psychology and counseling, I am not a psychologist and am not trying to go into any kind of detailed teaching on the different personality types, nor will I give an exact definition of what I mean by "emotional personalities." My assumption is that if you have one you will know it, and no one needs to define it for you.

Both the emotions and thinking skills are gifts from God and He wants us to use them both for His glory and the benefit of our fellow man. Both emotions and intellect can and should be developed to higher and higher levels of usefulness. We do not suggest that emotional people should excuse any hurtful behavior, but instead we want to give them the assurance that God has great plans for them and will give them grace and wisdom to change if they seek after it. And we do not suggest emotional people be complacent or lazy with their mind so that they fail to develop their mental capacities. Our minds can be trained to think better tomorrow than they do today.

Also, please accept the fact that this is not a typical Bible Study textbook with lots of notes and quotes. Rather it will use stories and characters from the Bible and modern life to illustrate a simple point: God loves to use emotional people.

As I stated above, some of you have been accused of being too emotional. I would suspect that those accusations have produced a wounding in your heart and that you have felt a certain amount of insecurity around people who were not "emotional"—people who seemed to have everything together. This book is especially for you. So please read and enjoy, and rise up to fulfill your awesome potential in God.

So go ahead! Be so emotional!

—BEN R. PETERS

Chapter 1

The Traditional Bad Rap

Andrea, our fifteen year old daughter, let out a blood-curdling scream and went running barefoot into the woods that surrounded our southwest Washington home, still screaming at the top of her lungs. I had just informed her that Brenda and I had decided to have our little apricot poodle, Pancho (about her age), put to sleep by the vet. She knew this was coming, but was not emotionally prepared for this moment. He had always been there, as long as she could remember.

I had planned on taking our deaf, half-blind, arthritic dog to the vet on my way to a scheduled appointment in town. By the time I had found Andrea and calmed her down, I didn't have the extra time to stop at the vet. Poor little Pancho had a temporary reprieve. But a few days later, Pancho was resting under our car when I backed out of our driveway. He was too deaf to hear the car and quickly passed on into "Doggy Heaven."

Andrea is one of the most emotionally-expressive members of our family, but not the only one. Brenda, my wife, is also extremely expressive with her emotions. She has shared her testimony in many conferences and retreats, publicly acknowledging how often she got herself into all kinds of trouble because of her spontaneous and emotional nature.

We want to clearly state that not all emotionally expressive people are women. We have numerous examples of emotionally expressive men as well, both in Scripture and in contemporary life. But let me share a little about these two particular emotionally expressive people that God has personally blessed me with.

Andrea, who is still my little baby girl in her twenties, has been teaching drama and leading drama teams on ministry trips, both in North America and overseas. She has been to Eastern Europe twice, including Poland and the Ukraine. In Poland she taught drama and evangelism to young people from many nations. She has powerfully impacted many lives in her short time as an adult.

When Andrea was still a pre-teen, she began to enter and win competitions for dramatic poetry recitations. Our Christian School state conventions attracted many gifted contestants in this field. By eighth grade she was competing with high school girls including seniors. She took first place that year and the next four years as well.

Her mother, (who also happens to be my wife) Brenda, has deep compassion, bubbly enthusiasm and genuine generosity. Her ability to touch people's hearts with these positive gifts, has rapidly caused her to be in great demand as a speaker and as a personal friend and mentor. She has a platform presence that is natural and captivating. Yet she still has some of the struggles that are common to many people who are very emotionally expressive. Fears and anxieties, guilt and self-criticism, feelings of failure and inferiority have been frequent and intense. Through a variety of ways and means, which we shall discuss in a later chapter, God has set her free from much of the impact of these common companions of those who are emotionally expressive.

I could give many other examples, but the clear message I want to proclaim from the very outset is that emotionally expressive people can be tremendously effective in life and in the Kingdom of God. We must convey to all members of the Body of Christ, including the youth and younger children, that whether they have the I.Q. of Einstein and are totally non-emotional, or whether they are extremely emotional and not the least bit mathematical or scientific, or whether they have any combination of the above, they all have some wonderful gifts from God.

They each have a special destiny, and God gave them all the gifts and talents they need in order to make a great contribution to the Kingdom of God and to the people in their world.

The Problem

Over the years we have repeatedly heard statements that have used the general term "emotions" in a negative light. As a result those who see themselves as "emotional" may also see themselves in the same negative light. For instance, we've all heard the statement, **"You can't trust your emotions."** If emotions are portrayed as untrustworthy, then those who are very emotional may easily transfer that negative association to themselves.

At the same time, people who excel with their intellect, are consistently exalted and may tend to look down on those who respond more with their emotions than just cool logic. **They are seldom if ever told, "You can't trust your intellect."** Scripture does tell us, however, not to lean on our own understanding (Proverbs 3:5). Our understanding, it seems to me, relates more to our mind or intellect than to our emotions.

The fact is that although it is at least partly true that you can't trust your emotions, the same holds true for our intellect. In every part of God's creation we find very intelligent people arguing with each other. Whether it is politics or religion or which basketball team is the best, people will use their intellect to reason to opposite conclusions. Within the Body of Christ, people debate about so many doctrines, all using the same Bible as their proof. If we could trust our intelligence, then bright scholars from all the denominations should agree on their theology.

Scripture also makes so many other statements that remind us not to trust in anything but God. David said that he had more understanding than his teachers because he meditated on the word of God. Being rather emotional, himself, David learned to trust his relationship to God more than his own mind. When he made a decision to go to war, he didn't just consult with his generals; he sought the Lord and listened to the words of the prophets.

The problem is that while the assets and potential of the intellectually superior are reinforced throughout their lifetime, the assets and potential of those with strong emotions are often totally ignored or belittled. And yet, as we will clearly show, these people often make the greatest and most powerful contributions to society and the Kingdom of God.

Let me state it this way: **The potential for fulfillment and powerful impact in our world and in God's Kingdom is every bit as great for those with strong emotions as for those with great intellectual gifting.**

Our desire is that every precious child of God will discover his or her awesome potential to be powerfully used by Him. We will reveal why Satan has such an interest in putting down and keeping down those with strong emotional personalities. These people may well be the greatest threat to his kingdom and he desperately wants to keep them out of the action.

Perhaps you are one of those people who have been told to get a grip and not be so emotional? Have you ever felt that people who were more intellectual and less emotional were somehow better people than you, and had much more to offer their friends, family, job or church? Have you ever thought or been told that if you were less emotional, you wouldn't get into trouble the way you do, and you wouldn't cause so many problems for others?

If your answer to these questions is "yes," then this book is especially dedicated to you. On the other hand, if you have a spouse or a child or a special friend that you might call an emotional person, then this book is also a very important resource for you. God wants to equip you not only to accept someone wired differently than you, but also to help to empower that person to be all that they can be for their family, their work and their service to the Kingdom of God.

Disclaimer

Please understand that **I am in no way implying that all people who are emotionally expressive are less intelligent than those who are not.** Many emotionally gifted people also have great intellectual strength. But

society has tended to make emotional people feel less intelligent, even if they are not.

At any rate, we want to honor and empower those who are "emotional," regardless of their apparent I. Q. Even if their I. Q. (which only measures certain aspects of intelligence) is on the low side, they can still use their emotional energy in powerful ways for the Kingdom of God, and they should never feel inferior to others just because they are emotionally expressive. Rather, they should get excited about the awesome gifts that God has given them and do everything possible to develop those gifts to the max.

1. Society's Built-In Bias

All human beings who come into the world are quickly impacted by the value system of their culture. They are observed and evaluated according to certain aspects of their being. Note the following value system of our western culture:

- **Physical Appearance:** When a baby transitions from the womb to the world, the first thing we notice is its physical appearance. A person's physical appearance will always be one of the most noticed characteristics as he or she grows up. Both the changeable and the unchangeable characteristics will affect the way people perceive and treat him or her.
- **Emotions:** Very quickly, however, the little

person's personality begins to be revealed and his or her emotions become noticed and analyzed. Family members may notice a bad temper, or a cheerful disposition, a stubborn streak or a giving nature. He or she may be either passive or aggressive. Emotions are well-developed and observable at a very early age, although some emotional traits may not appear until later.

- **Intelligence:** Before long, however, it becomes obvious to the doting parents that this little son or daughter is not only handsome or beautiful, and sweet and precious, but he or she is also a budding genius. They are totally amazed at how fast this little wonder is learning so many new things. From this point on the child's level of intelligence will become increasingly important to most people as opposed to his or her emotional makeup and character.

Appearance, emotional makeup and intelligence are the three most observed attributes of the average human being from infancy on. But as the child approaches and enters the world of formal education, a major reinforcement of the superior value of intelligence takes place. Physical appearance will always affect the way others evaluate him or her, but intelligence will become more and more important, while emotional qualities will usually not be rewarded in any significant way.

Rewards for Academic Achievement

A. Honor

Very quickly, the child who has already been told that he or she is really smart will discover that academic achievement will get great rewards. From kindergarten to college, the academically bright students will receive honor after honor. Often they will be asked to be the teacher's helper, a great honor to a little person. Of the few things I do remember about my earliest days in school, most of them have to do with compliments I received for reading skills and academic achievement. I certainly enjoyed to the full every honor that came through such accomplishments. At the same time, no one was rewarded in any tangible way for any positive emotional contribution. They would have been punished however, when negative emotions were displayed.

For example, the effervescent student who brought joy and laughter to others in the class was not honored in any way. The child who showed compassion and love to the social misfits, like my wife often did, was never given a gold star or a public pat on the back. But if anyone started a fight because they were reacting to emotional pain which had been inflicted on them, they received strong discipline. In other words, positive emotions went unrewarded, but negative emotions were given great attention. The obvious, yet subtle, implication is that it's not too cool to be emotional.

Report cards play an important role in confirming this basic life value. They express a child's worth in terms of academic achievement. Those who do not attain to the inner circle of the "smart kids" must try to find their worth in social behavior, or more likely, social misbehavior. When the less mentally-gifted student comes home with his or her report card, they are usually given a lecture. The end result is that they have a reinforced feeling that if they are not achieving academically on someone else's level, then they are of less value to anyone, including God.

The greatest reinforcement to this value system probably comes mostly from the many little events that the child is a part of. People often praise the academically gifted child in front of peers and other adults. But there is usually no corresponding praise for the non-academically gifted child. He or she may be very gifted in other areas, such as showing love and kindness, serving sacrificially, and bringing a joyful atmosphere to an individual or group of people, but those qualities are less rewarded with public or private honor.

B. Money

It doesn't take long to discover that the money trail of life finds its biggest source in academic achievement. It may start out with $5.00 for every "A" on the report card. It goes on with scholarship money, which the very smartest in the graduating class usually monopolize. Although there are a variety of different qualities rewarded, it is academic achievement that takes the bulk of the scholarship money.

In addition, all through school, students are told that they will never make much money if they don't do well in school and go on to college and get some degrees. If they are satisfied with digging ditches, or living off of welfare, driving old cars, living in a shack and never amounting to anything in life, then they can skip the academic achievement. But if they want to be successful and financially prosperous, they had better be very gifted or make up for it with huge amounts of sacrifice to get good grades.

Once in college or university, the competition increases. To get the promise of a really great job or position, students must excel and produce a very impressive academic profile. Again, those who do not have the gifting to do that, usually accept the fact that the "brains" in the class will get the most lucrative careers, and provide a better living for their families.

Let me make this very clear. I am not against rewarding academic achievement and hard work. I simply want to bring some balance, by bringing honor, hope and encouragement to those God has gifted with strong emotional energy. I say that it's time we gave honor to those who have used their emotional energy for others and for the

Kingdom of God. As we will see in a later chapter, some of the greatest achievers have been very emotional people.

Again we want to repeat the fact that many who are very emotional also have a high degree of intelligence. Some of it may manifest in academic achievement, but some of it may manifest in the more right-brained creativity, that brilliant left-brained people may never hope to attain to. We all have talents and gifts from God, but none of us has greater value to God just because our gifts are more recognized by others. We are all very valuable to the Kingdom of God, and God joyfully accepts everything we give to Him from a heart of devotion and love.

Negative Rewards of Being Emotional

A. Dishonor

While the positive aspects of the emotional personality may be taken for granted, the negative responses will attract plenty of attention. Whether it is losing his or her temper, or being extra-sensitive to offenses (resulting in self-pity, or some other negative emotional reaction), it will never go unnoticed.

The response to such negative emotional behavior will usually be a statement like one of these:

"You're just too emotional."

"Would you just get a grip and use your head for a change?"

"Your reaction is totally illogical."

"Think about what you're going to say or do, before you get all emotional and weird."

"When are you going to learn to control your emotions?"

In all of these responses, the person who lacks understanding for the emotional person keeps on reinforcing the idea that being emotional is a bad thing. "If you want to be a good person," he implies, "you have to stop being emotional, and be logical like me." This, of course, is like a leopard trying to remove his spots. It's probably not going to happen. Instead, the emotional person continues to get a lower and lower self-image, and has no idea how valuable his or her emotional energy is to God and His Kingdom.

B. Poverty (Material, Spiritual and Moral)

This repeated attack by non-emotional people on the personal worth of those with emotional personalities, leads to an acceptance of the lie that they will never be very successful in life, because of this unconquerable handicap. We have no idea how much damage this has done to millions of people world-wide, including those in the Christian Church.

The way we think affects the way we act and live. Those who feel they are of little value will probably contribute less, with the result that they will receive less in exchange. For a variety of reasons, we have millions of people in our western culture, subsisting on very little income, with no vision or hope of changing their lot in life, even though they have great latent potential, and a variety of opportunities to improve their lot.

Many of these are those unfortunate souls who feel that they were dealt a bad hand, because their academic abilities were not as strong as others. It is true that many have suffered from environmental trauma, which has helped to handicap their vision and hope. But if they were to receive enough encouragement from caring people who could see their potential and convince them that they had other valuable gifts to offer, many of these would achieve great things in their life.

The greatest tragedy is not the loss of financial gain, but the loss of spiritual accomplishments. When people feel that God can only use them in a limited way compared to others, they will close their ears to the higher call of God for their lives. They will live as spiritual paupers, never finding victory or fullness of joy that God has desired for them to enjoy, and they will never discover the fulfillment of doing the great exploits for God that He wants them to enjoy.

Another form of poverty accepted by many is moral poverty. This applies to all, but especially to females. Many, who feel that they are just "Dumb Blondes" decide to make the best of a bad situation and take advantage of what physical assets that they have to make themselves accepted and loved. Soon, they are taken advantage of and lose their self-respect and moral purity.

Young men, who feel like the class "Dummy" may feel that they can't achieve success the way others do, so they will accept the lie that they must compensate by being the class clown or by bullying or cheating. They man soon find themselves in trouble with the law, or in situations where they are using and abusing others for their own gratification. Both young men and young women could be spared much of their pain, if someone convinced them that they were just as valuable and precious as the academically superior people in their world.

Chapter 2

Oh God, What Have You Made?

*M*illions of people, including Christians, have asked God the above question. If God was truly all-powerful and loving, how could He have made me the way I am? Our focus in this book is on the emotional make-up, rather than physical appearance, but people ask the same question for both aspects of God's creativity. Many have cried out to God and asked Him why He made them so emotional. They don't see why they have been handicapped with such strong emotions, which so often get them into trouble and make them feel totally weak and worthless.

One of the most important truths related to the subject of this book is the truth that each one of us has received gifts from God to give us a very important function in the body of Christ. No one is left out. We have received both natural and spiritual gifts. Each list of spiritual gifts has an "each one" attached.

Let's look at what some of the greatest men in the Bible had to teach us about this principle:

Paul

Paul fills most of I Corinthians 12, which lists the nine "manifestation gifts," with his great teaching on the body of Christ. He clearly states, and then restates, the truth that everyone is very important in the body of Christ. Each one is important because God has given everyone gifts that give them their place and function in His body.

In fact Paul makes it clear that those parts which have less public honor are given special treatment to compensate. Now please read carefully what Paul declared earlier in this letter to the Corinthians:

"For you see your calling, brethren, that **not many wise** according to the flesh, **not many mighty, not many noble,** are called. But **God has chosen the foolish things** of the world to put to shame the wise, and God has chosen **the weak things** of the world to put to shame the things which are mighty; and **the base things** of the world and **the things which are despised** God has chosen, and **the things which are not,** to bring to nothing the things that are, **that no flesh should glory in His**

26

presence" (I Corinthians 1:26-29).

If we believe the Bible, we must confess that each of us is special in the eyes of God, and those who are looked down on by man are given special favor by God. When Jacob preferred Rachel over his other wife, Leah, God favored Leah and gave her four sons before her sister Rachel had any children. He did the same basic thing for Peninah, the wife of Elkanah, who was also the husband of Hannah, the mother of Samuel. If you have been put down because you are more emotional than intellectual, then rejoice, because God has an awesome blessing for you. Remember, **God's favor and anointing are the great equalizers.**

David

David also, in many of his Psalms, declared that God cares about the underdog and the one who is looked down on by his peers. He was the extreme underdog in his family. His father didn't even think of him as a possible candidate for the throne, and his seven older brothers despised him. He was chased from cave to cave by King Saul, and yet he was exalted to the position of King of all Israel. His gifts were not recognized by those closest to him, but they were recognized by God. And so are yours!

Joseph

Joseph was favored by his father, but hated by his brothers. He was sold into slavery and then placed in prison.

But his Heavenly Father intervened, and through the anointing which empowered his God-given spiritual gifts, he became the chief administrator of the most powerful nation on earth, after first being a slave and a prisoner in Egypt. I repeat again; God's favor and anointing are the great equalizers. And we know that God is no respecter of persons. What He has done for others, He can do for you.

Four Lepers

Talk about underdogs! No one would expect deliverance from famine and starvation to come from four total outcasts who lived just outside the city walls. But God chose the things which were despised by man to amaze the King of Samaria and the whole city. The lepers were the lowest human beings on the totem pole, but God used them to bring the "gospel," the "good news," that delivered the whole besieged city from starvation. If God can use such outcasts of society, He can also use us, no matter what other people think about us.

Finding our Place in His Body

It is definitely a truth that sets us free. We were not created to be just like anyone else in the body of Jesus. He made me different and unique, just like He made you. I can be mentored and receive someone else's mantel, but I will never be just like anyone else on the earth. I have a unique combination of gifts and talents and my heredity and environment have formed me into something unlike anything that there has ever been on the earth or ever will be.

God knew this when He created me, and prepared a path and a calling for me that was designed specifically for what I am. And that wonderful destiny is interwoven with the destiny of many other members of the body of Christ. His plan was that we all become members of His team, with each of us finding and filling our specific role on the playing field.

Only God could coordinate the different gifts and talents, personalities and character traits and design a destiny for each one which will flow in awesome harmony with the destinies of so many other unique individuals. Our job is to truly discover who He made us to be and with whom He wants us to flow. No matter who on earth has rejected us, He still has the same awesome destiny for us to make a powerful impact on our world.

As we will see in future chapters, the person with the predominantly emotional make-up has tremendous potential to impact his or her world.

Chapter 3

God's Hall of Fame is Full of Emotional People

GOD IS AN EMOTIONAL BEING

*I*t doesn't take much Bible reading to discover that God, Himself, is a being with both intelligence and emotion. It is fitting then that being made in His own image, human beings would have a mixture of both. God expressed great emotion in many parts of Scripture in His dealings with His people and the nations of the world.

In various places God expresses sorrow, joy, anger, jealousy and passionate love. From the stories of Adam and Eve to the conclusion of all things in Revelation, we experience God's emotional dealings with His creation. From His expressions of anger with His people in the wilderness, to the Lamentations of Jeremiah, God allowed His people to see

His own emotional nature. If God is not just pure intellect, but also emotional, and still runs the universe, then perhaps it's O.K. for us to be emotional beings as well.

Let's now look at some of the more emotionally expressive people in Scripture. Our information is limited about most of the men and women of the first two millennia. We know that Cain got emotional enough to kill his brother, Abel, but the Genesis record does not report much detail for this study until the time of the patriarchs.

JACOB

Probably the most emotional of the three Hebrew patriarchs was Jacob. He was not only emotional, but he had some definite character weaknesses. And yet God chose him to be the one that the nation of Israel would be named after. His grandfather, Abraham, and his father, Isaac, each had only one son of promise, but Jacob had 12 sons of promise and through him, God's "chosen people" began to multiply on the earth.

Jacob was very passionate about his love for Rachael. He is a great example of dedication and commitment, working fourteen years for the privilege of marrying his chosen bride. But he also gained fame by "wrestling with the angel" until he had the blessing he wanted. Jacob was ambitious and passionate with both positive and negative emotions and character traits, but he overcame his weaknesses and went on to establish the people of God as a nation on the earth.

MOSES

Moses is one of the greatest examples of an emotional personality that God powerfully used on the earth. The Bible records much about Moses, which reveals both his strengths and weaknesses. He was called the meekest man on the earth, but he also struggled with insecurity, anger, self-pity and depression.

Moses killed an Egyptian in an emotional response to watching a fellow-Hebrew being beaten. He then fled in fear to the wilderness, where his kindness to strangers won him favor with his future father-in-law, Jethro. But when God appeared to him in a burning bush and gave him a call to ministry, Moses revealed his fear, insecurity and feelings of inferiority. He continued to argue with God until God struck a deal with him, allowing him to use his brother Aaron as a spokesman for him.

Several times Moses complained to God about his job and the people God had given him to guide through the wilderness. Self-pity was no stranger to this mighty leader. Anger surfaced again when Moses struck the rock, to which God had only instructed him to speak. God disciplined him by not allowing him to enter the Promised Land.

But Moses also had a passion for the presence of God. The experience with the burning bush put a desire in his heart for more. He spent more than one forty-day session on the mountain with God, ignoring any desires for food or drink. He told God that without His presence, he didn't want to go on, and then asked for a special favor from God. He wanted to see God's glory in a way no man had ever seen it before. God granted his desire.

Moses also had great compassion for the people that he led. On one occasion God was threatening to totally wipe them out and make Moses the father of a multitude of people. Moses cried out to God for them and offered to have his own name blotted out of God's book on their behalf.

God honored Moses in powerful ways. The coming of Jesus was the fulfillment of a prophecy that God would raise up a prophet like Moses. In another passage, God said that Moses was much more than a prophet. Prophets would be given dreams and visions and dark sayings, but Moses talked with God face to face.

Moses was probably the most honored man by the Jews in Jesus time. Along with Abraham and David, Moses had tremendous respect from all the people of Israel as the one who brought them out of bondage with signs and wonders and the one who gave them the law of God.

Moses was one of the greatest men in all of biblical history, but he was also one of the most emotionally expressive. His words were powerful and inspired the children of Israel to follow him for forty years through the wilderness. Although some rebelled, the several million Israelites never returned to Egypt, as the rebels wanted them to do. And when Moses died, the people mourned for him like they would have mourned for their own father, for he truly was a father to them all.

HANNAH

Hannah appears to have been an extremely emotional gal. Being the most loved wife of Elkanah, God allowed her to be barren until she made God a deal and offered her first-born son to the Lord, if He would just give her one. Before the Lord opened her womb, we have the record that she wept bitterly about her barrenness. She was in such grief of spirit that her husband could not cheer her up. She was continually provoked to jealousy and appears to not really have had it all together to the natural eye.

But God loved her determination, desire and passion. Even though His high priest, Eli, misjudged her and accused her of being drunk, she passionately sought God for an answer. God gave her the answer, and God gave Israel a Samuel, who powerfully led Israel in the right paths for many years. After anointing Saul and watching him lose his favor with God through disobedience, Samuel was sent by God to anoint the greatest earthly king that ever ruled on the earth, who was also the forerunner of Jesus.

DAVID

Jesus was often referred to as the son of David. It was not because David was a perfect human being. He also had weaknesses and let his emotions and character faults get him into trouble. His sin with Bathsheba, and his pride in wanting to number his people brought great judgment and trouble into his life.

And yet he was called, "A man after God's own Heart" and "The sweet Psalmist of Israel." His passion for God was rivaled by very few. His own heart "panted after" the heart of God.

David expressed emotions repeatedly. His Psalms are filled with passion. He cried out to His God in distress, and despair. He also expressed more joy than any other character in Scripture. He longed for God's presence and His power to be revealed. David danced before the Lord in the presence of all Israel, to the embarrassment of his more sophisticated wife. But he told her bluntly that he would be even more undignified than that in his worship of the Lord.

David was about as emotional as anyone in Scripture, but there was never any doubt that he was also an effective and powerful leader. Let the reader be encouraged that David's emotional nature, although it got him into some trouble, also was greatly used by God to powerfully impact the destiny of his nation and the whole world for all of eternity. David learned not to limit God. His intimacy with God produced powerful faith.

David's faith in God led him into battle with Goliath and the Philistine armies. He never doubted his authority over the enemies of Jehovah. His faith led others to follow him into battle and to desire him to be their king. His confidence in the God he knew intimately and emotionally led him into the conquest of all neighboring nations, until they were all paying tribute to Israel. When his son, Solomon, took the throne, he had nothing to fear from any potential enemies, and he was free to focus on building the temple of the Lord.

King David ushered in the Golden Age of Israel. It did not begin with a Harvard or Yale law school education. It did not begin in a military academy where he learned the art of swordsmanship. Rather, it began in the fields watching his father's sheep. It began with a heart that was yearning to know His God. It began with tears of desperation to have divine encounters with the creator of the universe and the lover of his soul. Through his intimacy with His God, his faith and love and joy increased proportionally and while he maintained this intimate relationship nothing on earth was able to take away his confidence in His God. The lion and the bear were taken out with the same faith in God that he took out the nine-foot Goliath.

JEREMIAH

All the prophets expressed emotion, but Jeremiah was the only one known as "The Weeping Prophet." He expressed overwhelming emotion at the destruction of Jerusalem and felt the pain both of God's heart and of the people who were being judged for forsaking their God. Jeremiah wrote the whole book of Lamentations, which is a poetic book describing the pain and suffering that he felt deeply for his people.

Jeremiah, the emotional prophet, was a prophet to the nations, and spoke in the presence of several kings. Some invited him into their secret chambers to ask the word of the Lord. King Zedekiah wanted to hear what God was speaking, although he refused to obey the advice he received.

Jeremiah was also the one who prophesied the seventy-year time of captivity. It was the prophecy which Daniel would later read and take courage from. It inspired him to go into intercession for the fulfillment of Jeremiah's prophecy. As a result, men like Ezra and Nehemiah were dispatched by Cyrus and other later emperors to rebuild the temple and the walls of Jerusalem, and to lead their fellow Jews back to the land of the fathers.

Being emotional didn't stop Jeremiah from being used by God. In fact through his passion, many hearts and lives were touched and motivated to follow God.

PETER

The number one candidate for the "Most Emotional Person Award" in the New Testament would probably be Peter. This early church apostle was impulsive and very emotional, with many serious failures, but also many great accomplishments.

Peter went from "hero" to "goat" in fairly frequent fashion. He spoke words of revelation, complemented by Jesus, and then immediately spoke words which prompted Jesus to say, "Get behind me, Satan." He stepped out on the water before anyone else even thought of the wild idea. But very quickly his eyes were on the waves instead of Jesus, with the result that the sea and his body responded to the natural law of gravity and he lost his miracle.

My theory, which I can't prove from the Greek (or the Hebrew or the English for that matter), is that Peter's pride was actually what took his eyes off the Lord. My guess is that Peter felt so excited about his miracle of walking on the water that he just had to see if the other disciples were watching him. Of course, they were behind him in the boat, so he had to turn his head to see them. Just then his eyes noticed a ten foot wave heading his way and he lost his faith and began to sink. This story illustrates to me the principle of "Looking unto Jesus, the Author and Finisher of our Faith" (Hebrews 11:2). Peter allowed Jesus to "author" his faith but not to "finish" it. Listening to Jesus say, "Come!" and looking at His extended arms and smiling face was enough to "author" his faith. But by turning his head he didn't allow Jesus to be the "finisher" of his faith.

Later, Peter in typical "Peter fashion" made heroic promises that he would die for Jesus rather than forsake him, even if he was the only one. He did make one attempt to defend Jesus, using his sword to remove the ear of the servant of the high priest, but an hour or two later, he was denying he even knew Jesus. When he heard the rooster crow, he wept bitter tears of repentance and remorse.

But after that great failure, Peter once again took his place of leadership in the "Early Acts" church. He administrated the first prayer meeting and then he preached the first spontaneous message and conducted the first New Testament church "altar call", to which three thousand souls responded. Peter continued to lead the exploding church with his powerful anointing and charisma. With John at his side, he ministered healing to the cripple at the temple gate and followed up with his second spontaneous message. This time the number rose to five thousand disciples.

When Ananias and Sapphira tried to make "brownie points" through lies and deception, Peter administered "Divine Justice" to them both, one at a time, through a clear word of knowledge. He also was the spokesman before the Sanhedrin and the one to pronounce a warning of judgment to Simon the sorcerer.

Later, Peter, who had been bold as a lion, was rebuked by Paul for compromise and cowardice. His weakness had surfaced again decades after Pentecost. It was a reminder of his humanity, but it had not stopped him from leading a small band of total failures until they had become a powerful force to turn the world upside down.

Peter did not accomplish these things in his own strength. Rather, his weaknesses were constant reminders of his total dependency on God. Emotional people tend to have this advantage over cold, calculating personalities that seldom get themselves into trouble unnecessarily. But those who fail frequently know how totally dependent on God they really are, and as a result they may tend to cry out to God more often for His help and anointing.

JOHN

John was a quieter personality and not the type of leader that Peter was. He was happy to be just a participant in the action, rather than the leader. But he was known as "The disciple Jesus loved." His focus on love and relationship inspired the writing of his three epistles and his powerful gospel. John 3:16 is the most often quoted and memorized verse in the Bible and speaks of God's love to saints and sinners alike.

God chose John to survive serious persecution and to grow to a ripe old age to remind the church about God's love. He was also chosen to write the last book of the Bible to seal up the written Revelation of God to man.

MARY

We could talk about several different Mary's, who all were recorded weeping at various times. But let's focus on Mary, the sister of Martha and Lazarus. She not only was weeping at the grave of Lazarus, but she was one who poured out the perfume on the feet of Jesus and worshipped

Him with reckless abandonment. She was the one who sat at the feet of Jesus while her sister labored with the meal.

Mary's passion for Jesus was truly powerful and all-consuming. Jesus promised that because of her passionate and sacrificial show of love for Jesus, when she broke the alabaster box of perfume, her story would be told wherever the gospel was preached.

PAUL

Paul is always thought of as an intellectual theologian and he certainly was. He did however reveal that he had a very passionate side to him. He spoke several times of the fact that he wept and labored in travail for them. He had a passion for Israel and was willing to lay down his life for them. He was very zealous for God. In his time of ignorance he zealously persecuted the Christians. Later, he was even more zealous for the Kingdom of God and willing to lay down his life for Jesus.

Although Paul has a reputation of being very theological, he spoke often in emotional terms. He asked the Philippians to fulfill his joy by being in unity. He wrote that he was weeping, even as he wrote about those who were unfaithful to their Heavenly calling. He taught about both the gifts and fruit of the Spirit. He warned us not to grieve or quench the Holy Spirit, being aware of the emotional sensitivity of the Third Person of the Trinity. He spoke both of the terror of the Lord and the constraining power of the love of Christ, both in the same chapter.

Paul had a very balanced personality and used both his mind and emotions to present and reveal Jesus to his audiences and to those who would read his letters. What he would say to those who are super-intellectual is: "It's all right to express your emotions. Just line up your emotions with the emotions of the Lord. Love what He loves and hate what He hates. Rejoice with Him when He rejoices and weep with Him when He weeps."

JESUS

As good an example as Paul was, there is none better than Jesus who was human and divine at the same time. And if we can show that Jesus freely expressed his emotions, then we can also be confident that there is a godly way for us to be emotional as well.

Jesus, our divine example showed his emotions on many occasions. He expressed intense passion, accompanied with anger, when He drove the money changers out of the temple. He showed grief and sorrow when he wept over Jerusalem, and also when he prayed in the Garden of Gethsemane. Jesus wept when he surveyed his friends, Mary and Martha, weeping along with many others, as they made their way to the tomb of Lazarus. The writer of Hebrews declared that He is our High Priest, who is touched with the feelings of our infirmities. He feels our pain! Isaiah said that He was a man of sorrows and acquainted with grief.

We have no record of Jesus laughing or joking, but He did talk about His desire that we would have His joy and that our joy would be full. I think we can assume that He did laugh and smile and even joke with His disciples. He certainly brought great joy to thousands of people as he healed their sick and set captives free. The lame and the blind found a new lease on life and their joy and the joy of their families must have known no bounds.

Jesus never discouraged people from expressing their emotions. Rather, He reminded them of the commandment to "Love the Lord your God with all your heart, with all your soul, with all your mind, and with all your strength." That commandment certainly implies to me that you can use your emotions to worship God and to love Him. In fact, it seems to me that not to use your emotions to worship God would be a violation of this commandment. We usually think of the soul as the mind, will and emotions. But even if you define the soul differently, the focus of the commandment is that we use everything within us to love and serve God. Leaving out our emotions would thus be a violation of that commandment.

Chapter 4

The Powerful Potential of Emotionally Expressive People

While cold and calculating intellectuals may design our bridges, airplanes, rocket ships and computers, it takes those who know how to impact the hearts and emotions of other people to rally a nation to go to war to defend their freedom, or to draw multitudes to Jesus in evangelistic meetings, or to bring healing to broken hearts or even to captivate the attention of a small child. Only emotionally expressive people can impact an audience with drama, music and other performing arts. Highly educated health care specialists can diagnose problems, perform extremely difficult surgeries and prescribe treatments, but it takes a warm and friendly smile and compassionate words to truly make the patient feel good.

There are so many ways that God can use our emotions to serve Him. Just a smile at the right moment can make a difference in someone's life. An anointed emotional message can motivate a multitude to rise up and take action. A compassionate hug or an arm around the shoulders can give strength to go on, and as we have seen so often, a stirring prophetic word to a suicidal man, woman or young person can change the natural and eternal destiny of that emotionally wounded soul.

I have watched my wife minister with great feeling and compassion to many people of different ages, reminding them that God loved them and that He was aware of their feelings that things might be better if they weren't around. One night in a small meeting in Nevada two suicidal bikers had their hearts changed because of the gripping word that Brenda shared with them individually. One of them looked her in the eye after the meeting and told her she needed to know that he had planned on taking his life that very night. His loaded gun was already under his pillow ready to be used to end his earthly existence. It wasn't just the prophetic word that impacted him and the other man. It was also the sincere love and compassion that came through her to their soul and spirit.

Music

The story is told of a musician who heard a performance by a young female opera singer. He knew she had the talent but lacked the passion to be as great as she could be. He made advances toward her until she fell in love with him. Then he broke her heart by leaving her. Her singing was powerfully affected by the experience. Every note and every word was colored by deep emotion and the crowds were deeply touched by her performance.

Music plays an incredibly important part in our lives. Many of us are used to being surrounded by music much of our day. Music motivates us, soothes us, comforts us and can be used as a vehicle to bring us into the presence of God. Music speaks the language of the soul and must touch our emotions. With being accompanied by some kind of emotion, few, if any, will want to listen to it.

People who are emotionally expressive may find music one of the ways that God can use them to impart His grace to others. I remember well one occasion at a Christian School Student Convention in Ellensburg, Washington. I heard a violin performance by a young lady still in high school. She had written an original arrangement of "His Name Is Wonderful."

Although I had heard the same girl perform a more technically difficult piece the previous year, I had never heard anything as spiritually impacting as this one. Very quickly I was taken into a realm of God's presence that I have seldom experienced. It was like she had taken me to Heaven and back. It is true that the violin is a very expressive instrument, but without the emotional input of the musician, it could hardly have had the impact that it had on me in that day.

Not long ago we were in the city of Inchon, South Korea, in a large Methodist church. I was scheduled to speak in just a few minutes, when the worship leader led the congregation in a joyful song that we recognized by the melody as one we knew in America. When we finished singing, the keyboard player and violin player continued to play the same song, but to a much slower tempo.

The anointing that emanated from the now mournful music took me into a vision. I saw myself with others at the Wailing Wall in Jerusalem. I felt the pain and passion of the people who longed for the restoration of their natural inheritance. I knew God was talking to me. I asked God to confirm it in His Word if He wanted me to change my message. I opened up my Bible and my eyes fell on Psalm 126 and I read, "They that sow in tears shall reap in joy."

A few minutes later I was in the pulpit, looking down over the crowd. I asked the violinist to stand. I told her that she had prophesied on the violin and that God had given me a brand new message because of the way she had used her gift and anointing for the Kingdom of God. She began to weep. I preached what I believe was one of the most powerful messages I had ever delivered from God to man. God gave me the message, including personal illustrations that made the message come alive. The response was incredible. The anointing at the altar touched at least two hundred precious souls, including the violinist, who was experiencing a powerful encounter with God.

The passionate release of God's anointing through a musical instrument impacted the guest speaker and hundreds of people. Divinely inspired and empowered emotions played a powerful role in the drama that night.

Public Speaking

Historians have declared that the speeches of Winston Churchill did more to win World War II than the prowess of the military power of Great Britain. How could the words of one man win a military battle?

Hollywood has dramatically captured the power of a leader to inspire armies to fight for their freedom and their national pride. Mel Gibson's roles in various war movies depict the power of passionate speech to motivate men to lay down their lives for their cause.

Churchill's many speeches inspired the British to believe that they could win the war. His famous, "We shall fight them on the beaches, we shall fight them in the air, we shall fight them on the landing grounds. . . .We shall nevaah surrendaah." was just one of the highly motivating speeches which were broadcast frequently on BBC radio. The local citizens and the military alike put tremendous energy into the war effort and their stubborn resistance broke the back of the German war effort. Wave after wave of the famous German "Blitzkrieg" had kept firefighters and civilians struggling to put out the terrible fires, but they wouldn't quit because their courageous leader repeatedly spoke passionate words of encouragement to them.

Most Americans know the story of Patrick Henry, a man who declared to all that no matter what others thought about the oppression of the British, his philosophy was, "Give me liberty, or give me death!" Through his passionate speech and through others like him, who cared fervently for freedom, leaders from the colonies laid their lives and fortunes on the line to bring political freedom to America.

Speaking is, of course, an obvious way to serve God. Some will speak to millions like African evangelist Reinhard Bonnke. Others will speak just as passionately to only a few on a street corner or in a home meeting. The results could be the salvation of one precious soul or more than a million in one meeting.

Those who have heard Reinhard Bonnke preach know that he does not speak without passion and emotion. His message is, of course, reinforced through the powerful testimonies of miraculous healings, but the passion of the delivery of his message holds the attention of millions of needy people at the same time.

Drama

The ability to act dramatically is the ability to feel emotion and express it before an audience. All of our five children have been used by God in one form of drama or another. Brenda and I also enjoyed a bit of acting in school many years ago, although those experiences were not necessarily for the glory of God.

Today, drama teams, like those sent out by the Dallas-based, Christ For the Nations Institute, travel to other cities and nations and perform on streets and city plazas. Children and adults alike gather to watch and then listen as the message is presented through the drama, mime and the preaching which follows. Our daughter, Andrea, as we mentioned earlier, has been to Eastern Europe twice with the CFNI drama team, and has seen a tremendous harvest as a result. Many people have responded to the salvation invitation.

Willow Creek Community Church, one of America's largest churches, uses drama in every main weekend service, setting the stage for Pastor Bill Hybels' message. Thousands of souls have come to Christ through this church, and many emotionally expressive folk have found a way to use their gifts for the Kingdom of God.

Other folk find their way into the professional theatre, television and movies. Today, Hollywood is being invaded by Christian actors and actresses, producers and writers, who want to influence their world for good and for the

Kingdom of God. Other famous performers are being converted and cleaning up their acts. While most movies and modern television shows are becoming more and more corrupt, others are setting a higher standard and are becoming a positive influence in the land.

Other Art Forms

Some people express themselves in other art forms such as painting, photography, writing (including poetry), sculpture and dance. All of these can employ divine creativity to speak to other people and all of these are usually an expression of emotion and create an emotional response. Some people find full-time employment with these art forms, but most people are blessed just find a fulfilling way to serve God and His people.

Many individuals are not aware of latent talents and gifts from God. My younger sister, Carrie, did not have any great talent in art as far as I was concerned, while growing up with her. But after being a mother for many years, she began to do some oil paintings. Artists who saw her work recommended she set a high price tag. Her first picture was sold for $1,000. She sold many more after that, including some to local politicians, until she and her husband opened an art store and art gallery along with some other artists in a community near Owen Sound, Ontario, Canada.

I would encourage people who are expressive with their emotions to get out and join some kind of a class to see what they might be able to do with some of their latent abilities. It's a lot better than just watching others use their skills on T.V. or listening to their music and observing their artistic abilities. Just tell God that whatever talents you discover and develop will be dedicated to Him for His glory. Then when things go well for you, don't forget that covenant with Him.

Intercession

You don't have to be emotional to be an intercessor, but most intercessors do tend to be emotional. God delights in emotional intimacy with His children, and with His chosen Bride, the Church of Jesus. I would never underestimate the things that have been accomplished through the fervent prayers of God's people.

Many pastors and evangelists will be surprised in Heaven at how great the rewards of intercessors will be. The pastors and evangelists have in many cases received much of their rewards in the praise of men, especially if that's what they sought for. But the intercessors have prayed in secret for their pastors and evangelists. Much of the fruit will be credited to their account and their rewards will be exceedingly great.

A modern opportunity for those who love to pray for people is to answer phone calls for people who call in for prayer in response to various Christian radio or television programs. Some are calling for salvation and others are calling for a variety of other human needs. But who better to fill such positions than those who really know the heart of God and know how to pray!

How does one become an intercessor?

First, start praying daily for the "burden of the Lord." Acknowledge your humanity and how easily you are distracted by the "things of earth." Ask God to give you His heart and His passion. Ask Him what He loves and what He hates. Ask Him for the same emotions. Ask Him to help you rejoice when He rejoices and weep when He weeps. These are prayers He longs to hear and these are the prayers that He will give first priority to. I call them "Kingdom First Prayers," because they are not for our own immediate personal benefit.

Second, become intimate with the Bible. All intercessors should be lovers of the written Word of God. It is in the Bible that we have our greatest revelation of the heart of the Father. It was in His Holy Word that God gave me a burden for His Church, the Body of Christ. It was spending time absorbing the Scriptures that fanned the revival fires in my own spirit and caused me to pour out my soul on a daily basis as a nineteen-year-old Bible College freshman for the cause of genuine revival.

We could all pray more, but God is looking not for those who want to be more "spiritual", but for those who really want to know Him and be intimate with Him. He is looking for a heart like His own heart. His promise is that

He will show Himself strong on our behalf if we have that kind of a heart (II Chronicles 16:9).

Teachers

No one wants to be taught by someone speaking in a monotone—showing no emotion. Adults and children alike respond to expressive and dynamic teachers. If you are naturally expressive and show emotion when you speak, you could be a great teacher.

You need to have something to teach, of course, and you need to know what level you are more gifted for. You might be a teacher for pre-schoolers, or grade school kids or any level up to older adults or pastors and leaders. All are just as important to God. But you could find great fulfillment as a teacher, dedicating your gifts to God.

Ministries of Mercy

Many different applications of this category are available. You can use your emotional nature to bless both the young and old. You could minister in children's hospitals, in retirement and nursing homes. You could work for the Salvation Army or a local city mission. You could also help in a food bank or thrift store.

You can just be a person who shows mercy wherever you go. You can be one who laughs with those that laugh, and weeps with those that weep. You can give people encouraging words from the Lord, if you just take a little time to learn to listen to His voice.

You can take mission trips to various lands and love the children with your eyes and your smiles and your arms. You can help in medical missions with just a little training and your gentle spirit will be a great encouragement to others. And God won't miss one act of kindness, even though you don't do it on stage. His rewards for you will be far greater than any fame or fortune on the earth.

Secretaries and Receptionists

People, whose job it is to give information and direction to guests, can bless so many people if they have a vibrant, bubbly spirit. When people give accurate information and direction, some feel they have done their job. But when you add a warm friendly smile and warm friendly words, those who come for information will leave feeling like they just got a bonus from their boss.

Even a vibrant voice over the phone can change the atmosphere for someone who is depressed. One of the best examples I have experienced happened when I called the office of Bishop Bill Hamon, the director of Christian International. Both of his secretaries have the most cheerful and kind voices that one could ask for over the phone. It was definitely a Godly grace that could not be taken the wrong way. It was certainly an encouragement to me and I have no doubt it has been an encouragement to thousands of others as well.

Food Servers and Ministers of Hospitality

Along with waiters and waitresses, those who invite people into their homes to show hospitality play an important role in our society. We have all had a variety of personalities serve us at tables. What a difference it can make to the enjoyment of our meal when the one who serves us is sweet and kind, thoughtful and responsive. On the other hand, a server with a sour disposition makes the food much less appetizing and the experience far less enjoyable.

Neither this author, nor our Heavenly Father would put a server of food into a category of any less value or importance than any other position available for service to God. After all, Jesus said that the greatest among us would be the servant of all. Many food servers are treated, even by Christians, as lower class citizens. Both my wife and two daughters have spent time in these positions, and they are extremely gifted in these areas because of their emotional, sensitive and expressive personalities. In my opinion, there are none better!

Administrators

Administrators may seem less likely to be in a position occupied by emotionally expressive people. But many such people are very organized as well as expressive. If you have the administrative gift and can perform it with sensitivity to the needs of the people you administrate, you will be much better qualified for the job than someone who just uses people as non-personal tools to complete a job.

People will much rather serve someone who shows them love and consideration than they would serve people who treat them rudely. When the pressure is on, employees or those who serve under the administrator will perform better if they know their service will be appreciated and rewarded with a smile, a hug or a "Great job!" I could give many personal illustrations, but I'm sure you probably have plenty of your own.

This list could go on and on, but I think I have made my point. When it comes to working with people, those who are emotionally expressive can outperform those who are not. And when it comes to serving the Lord in strategic intercession, it doesn't hurt to be emotional. Jesus was not ashamed to cry out to His Father and God certainly responded to His prayers.

Chapter 5

Maximizing the Positive and Minimizing the Negative

Defeating the "Defeatist" Mentality

People who are emotionally expressive often exist in a state of at least semi-defeat, because their negative emotions have made them feel like total failures, and they have not seen themselves worthy of any significant role in the Kingdom of God. People have been upset with them and they assume that God is as well.

**We may need to face the facts,
but we must embrace the truth.**

The fact is that we all mess up.

The truth is that God forgives totally and forgets our boo-boos.

The fact may be that we lost our temper.

59

The truth is that He will not despise a broken and a contrite heart.

The fact may be that others appear more talented than us.

The truth is that God has given gifts to each of us.

You'll find the phrase, "each one" at least seven times in the New Testament when referring to spiritual gifts. In Psalm 68:18, God declares that He gave gifts even to the rebellious, so that He, Himself, could dwell among us. He longs to use us and strengthen our faith in Him.

Satan's goal is to keep us feeling defeated so that we don't rise up and build the Body of Christ to its potential power. God's goal is to encourage us and strengthen us so that we can serve Him and bring in the harvest He is waiting for. A defeatist mentality is Satan's subtle devise to neutralize the army of God.

So, first of all, agree with God that you are special and have an important place in the body of Christ. You may have problems, but you also have gifts. And God will gladly use your gifts in spite of your problems. He will also show you how to receive help from Him. Often this help will come through others, but however it comes, the result will be to minimize or eliminate your weaknesses while you serve Him on the earth.

Dealing With Our Negatives

A few common weaknesses of emotionally expressive people are the following:

Self-pity: Sensitive personalities struggle the most with this one. This is such a subtle, but destructive emotion that can lead to many other problems. Don't be merciful on your flesh with this one. Deal with it quickly before it builds momentum and hurts you and others. Make no mistake— self-pity is your mortal enemy. It wants to reduce you to a victim of others in your own eyes and keep you spiritual paralyzed.

Anger: This one is the most obvious, and as we well know, it can be extremely hurtful. We need to accept total forgiveness from God, from those we hurt and from ourselves. Getting depressed will only harm everyone we love and ourselves too. In the following discussion, we will deal with some basic tools to defeat this enemy or our well-being and of our service to the Kingdom of God.

Fear: Fears can be totally disabling and immobilizing. God's Word makes it clear that fear comes from our enemy. We need to learn to attack the fear and panic with Scripture and prayer and help from our spiritual family. John told us that perfect love casts out fear, and we need to know how to appropriate that love into the deepest recesses of our soul, which may be hiding hurt and rejection from many years back.

Impulsiveness: This weakness can cause a variety of problems, especially in the area of finances, or weight gain. Self-discipline is so difficult for many emotionally expressive people who love the adventure of doing the unplanned and the emotionally appealing. This tendency may have some positive aspects to it, but it can also result in many types of disaster.

Immorality: Emotional people may have more problems with this terrorist than those who are less emotional. The reason is that they may become more easily aroused through romantic words or music or other aspects of atmosphere. They may have more trouble drawing the line when their emotions and passions are aroused. The consequences of a lack of self-control in this area can also be very devastating to a person's self-image and vision for the future.

Steps To Victory

How can one overpower these negative emotions and become the vessel unto honor that God can use in special places of service that we all desire? God's plan for us is that we gain the advantage over these things, and He wants us to know that He has provided all the tools to do so. Let's look at some of the things that will help us get the upper hand over these tormentors and thieves.

1. Face Your Weakness. Denial is often our worst enemy. Don't blame others. Own your problem long enough to deal with it. If you think it's always someone else's fault you can't do anything about it. But if you take responsibility for it, you have started on your way to victory. There are great books out on this subject, such as John Maxwell's

"Failing Foreword" and many others.

2. Humble Yourself To Ask For Help. God has gifts in the body to bring us all into a place of victory. We need each other and God wants us to build each other up with prayer and care. We're not the only one with problems. All Christians have their own, as well as gifts to help others over theirs. Remember that God gives grace to the humble and it is that divine grace that we need to conquer our weaknesses.

3. Renew Your Mind. Do this primarily with Scripture, but also with teaching tapes, worship music, and books and magazines that remind you of your destiny and bring you into the presence of God. Don't allow the old negative thoughts to come back to roost. Fill the nest of your mind with positive, faith-filled statements of God's love, and of His power over all the power of the enemy. Many people put Bible verses on their fridge or mirror or other places where they will often be seen. Whatever it takes, determine that you are going to change your way of thinking and develop a more scriptural mindset.

4. Develop Your Positive Gifts. In so doing, you will gain confidence that God can use you and it will help motivate you to stop doing things that will harm you and others and detract from your ministry. As mentioned earlier, take a class and try something that interests you that you've never done before. Read as many new books as possible. Ask others what would be good books to read in your area of interest. Ask God who you can be a blessing to and how. I believe we all have so many latent gifts that it would take about a thousand years to try to develop them all. In the light of this, we certainly don't need to waste time watching mindless television programs that just reprogram us to live in our negative world.

5. Focus More on Helping Others Than on Fixing Yourself. The more you focus on using your gifts in helping others, the more encouraged you will be about the fact that your life has purpose. Your outlook will be more positive and joyful. The more joy you have, the more strength you will have, because the joy of the Lord is your strength. That strength will help you to conquer the weaknesses of your flesh. Focusing too much on your weaknesses will make you look inward and probably make you more depressed and defeated.

6. Seek Godly Professional Help. If negative problems like anger or fear continue unabated, seek those with specialties in these fields. Some people have specialized gifts for certain problems, like doctors in the field of medicine. Be confident that there is someone in the Body of Christ who can help you. Don't give up! Keep asking God to lead you to your place of victory. Some deep inner healing may be what you need to get out the root of your problem and truly restore your soul.

7. Let Your Love For Jesus Overpower Your Weaknesses. This may be my last point, but it certainly is not the least. As a nineteen year old freshman in Bible College in Canada, I discovered a powerful principle of gaining victory over the flesh and the devil. Even today, when the flesh wants to rise up, I remind myself of this principle to build strength for victorious living.

I had been enjoying Bible School, and was eager to serve God, but was still experiencing defeat in at least one major battlefield with the flesh. When God asked me to humble myself and ask for prayer because of a lack of burden for others, that battlefield was not even on my mind.

God answered that prayer for His burden in an over-powering way. He began to give me such a passion for His church, that I began to spend many early morning hours crying out for revival and reading through the book of Acts over and over. My intercession was often very emotional with tears and weeping. My passion for God was so strong that before long it occurred to me that I was not experiencing defeat in that weak area of my life any more. Trying to conquer it with just prayer and determination had utterly failed. But when I opened my heart to the burden of the Lord and became His intercessor, my problem just evaporated.

I can illustrate this phenomenon by comparing it to a valley that has many little springs of water bubbling up and making little streams going in many different directions. They are like our desires, habits or weaknesses in our hearts and lives. Sometimes we want one thing, but later on we want something that will contradict the first thing. We yield to our second desire and then realize that we gave up something else that we wanted when we yielded.

For instance, you may have a strong desire to lose weight when you see your profile in the mirror. But the next day you are taken out to a buffet for dinner. Everything looks so good and your appetite desires to taste a little bit of everything. Later at night you look at your profile again and wish you had eaten much less.

What we have here are desires that are in competition with each other. In certain circumstances one desire is stronger than the other desires, but when the scene changes another desire gets the upper hand. How then do you bring the wrong desires under control?

Now back to the valley and its many little streams. If the rains came down from Heaven and the snow melted on the mountains and flowed down into that valley that was full of many little streams, something would happen that would change everything. Suddenly the valley would be one great river. All the little streams would become part of that one river. No little stream would be able to do its own thing. The flow of the river would determine the direction of every stream.

Even so, when we have one passion that fills our heart to overflowing, there is no other passion that can take control. Every minor passion must submit to the authority of the major passion of our heart. That passion for revival completely overpowered the other passion that had defeated me for so long.

While my experience may have been different than yours and others, I do believe we can all apply this principle. We can all ask God for more of His burdens and His heart. He loves to download information as well as passion from His heart to ours. He may give you a burden for a certain ministry or mission field, but He will certainly give you something that will give your life passionate purpose and an increase in the flow of His Spirit through you. This may be just what you need to get that edge in your battle with uncontrolled emotions.

Chapter 6

Finding Your Place on the Team

*I*f you're still with me to this point, you have hopefully come to understand some basic truths. First of all, emotions are a really good thing when we can properly control or direct them. Secondly, emotional people have just as great potential in the Kingdom as those who are not emotional or as those who are mental giants.

We have also learned some of the things that emotionally expressive people can actually do better than those who are not. In addition we looked at some of the ways we can conquer or minimize the damage done by negative emotions. I trust that we have clearly made the case that an emotionally expressive person can have a very fruitful and fulfilling and victorious life.

In this short and final chapter, we want to focus on the fact that whether you are very emotional or very unemotional, you are never going to really fulfill God's destiny for you unless you find your place on His team. It's not enough to have special gifts and talents and find ways to use them for God. Instead, God wants to position you in the best possible place on His team. When you are in that position you will find a release to spend the greatest part of your time doing what you do the best, while allowing others with different gifts to do what they do best.

Specialization

Professional sports teams are moving into more and more specialization. The field of medicine is becoming even more specialized with every passing year. The world of industry also knows the advantage of having leaders who specialize in one main area and work together with other leaders who can focus on a different area. That is the only way that a business can successfully compete with other companies.

Likewise the Kingdom of God was designed to grow rapidly. partly through the wise use of specialization. Paul taught us in I Corinthians 14, how important each different member of the body of Christ is to God and the rest of His body. Paul mentions the hearing and seeing and other functions of different parts of the body. All of the body parts are needed, even if some of them are out of sight and not in the public eye.

The human body is the perfect team. Each part does its part. Like the different special teams on a football club, the body has many systems for particular jobs. Our bodies have a skeletal system to give the body structure, a nervous system for communication from the brain to each member, a muscular system to enable movement, a cardiovascular system to pump the blood, a digestive system to break down food to feed the body, an immune system to help the body fight off disease, a reproductive system to make more of us and an elimination system to get rid of waste materials. I may have missed one or two, but you get the point. All of these systems must work together for the body to be healthy and accomplish its goals.

So it is in the body of Christ. You are a part of the body and a part of a team within that body. Just as there are different kinds of bones in the skeletal system and different muscles in the muscular system, so you are part of a team within a bigger team. It is your natural and spiritual gifts that give you your function in that body and your place on the team. You may be a good eye or ear or hand, but disconnected from the body, you do no good to anyone.

And apart from the rest of the team your athletic skills won't win any games. You may be a great running back, but if you aren't a functioning member of a football team no one cares if you score a touchdown when and where no one else is even playing. You need to become a member of the offensive backfield squad on an actual footfall team.

Even so, with all your emotional energy and gifts, you must find your place. God will help you if you ask Him. After all, it is Jesus' own body that we're talking about. The Father is looking at the body that Jesus has to use on the earth, and He wants something much better for His Son. You are a part of that body, and it will function much better if you are in the place where you will be the most productive, the place for which He specially designed you.

Partners in Ministry

Often God puts two people together in special working relationships as balancing team members in His body. This is usually as a husband/wife team, but it can be any two other people. God usually places opposite personalities together to balance each others' strengths and weaknesses. If you are highly emotional, you may be teamed up with someone who is much more logical and unemotional. This may cause some severe conflicts initially, but God wants each of us to humble ourselves to learn from each other. If we do, we will learn valuable things about other types of personalities and we will be protected from harm that would come our way from not getting the whole picture.

Emotional people may not want the discipline of having to get structured or organized. They may not want to have to balance their checkbook or live by a budget. But if they allow their organized partner to help them, they will avoid some serious consequences. At the same time, the more logical and organized person may not see the importance of being sensitive to other people's feelings or spending money on gifts that are not on his or her budget, but if he or she can be flexible enough to learn about different personalities, it will produce abundant blessings in the days and years to come.

My wife and I are a perfect example of the above statements. Brenda is extremely sensitive to other people's needs and feelings, while I like to be much more organized and much less spontaneous. If it wasn't planned, my instinct is that it should wait until we have more time to think about it. This is of course a real "kill-joy" attitude. But Brenda's greatest joy is giving and making other people feel good about themselves. She does it through kind words, often inspired by God, and through little things she gives away. At her ladies' retreats she always has special gifts for the ladies. So when she sees the opportunity to get something that would bless someone else, she wants it right now before it's too late or before it goes off sale.

This tendency has caused occasional stress on our finances, which gives me stress, because I pay the bills. But the end result is that the thousands of seeds of kindness that she has sown over the years are now reproducing thousands of folk that stand with us in our ministry, including some that provide critical financial support. It would not come in like it does is if it just depended on my teaching and preaching ministry. I believe most of our support comes in as a response to Brenda's wonderful gift of giving of time, energy and resources that says to people, "I love you," and "You are important to me and to God."

Leadership Involvement

As church leaders are learning more and more about their responsibility to equip the saints for the work of ministry, they will focus more and more on helping each member or partnership find their place in the body of Christ. Rather than just filling vacancies in their present work force, they will see creative new ways to tap the resources of the saints in order to reach out to more souls and bring in the abundant harvest that is already over-ripe.

For more information, I recommend my previous book, *Folding Five Ministries Into One Powerful Team*. In this book I share what I believe is God's master plan for putting all the basic ministries together to reach the world with the gospel in a powerful way.

Go For It and Don't You Dare Give Up and Quit!

One of the weaknesses of the emotional personality is the desire and tendency to feel so beat up and worthless and like such a failure that the only apparent option is just to give up and quit. That is exactly what you must not do. Your mountains are not as big as they appear, and your failures are not nearly as upsetting to God as they are to you. The devil is a liar and he wants you to believe that you will never succeed and be worth anything to anyone. The fact is that you can make every failure a steppingstone to a future success. Or as leadership expert, John Maxwell, calls it, you can "Fail Forward."

It's time for all of God's specially gifted emotional people to rise up to fulfill their destiny and refuse to lose. Satan is very much afraid of the powerful potential of all of God's emotionally expressive children. He knows how fast they can be empowered to do exploits and how much energy they can put into the expansion of the Kingdom of God to the disastrous detriment to his own evil empire.

You can do it! Your gifts will make room for you and they will help you find your place in the body of Christ. But you need to stir up those gifts for the Kingdom of God. Get out of your comfort zone and take some risks.

Paul noticed that Timothy was a bit timid about using his spiritual gifts and he exhorted him to stir up or fan the flame of his gifts and not to neglect them. After exhorting him to fan the flame of his gifts, Paul declared, "For God has not given us the spirit of fear, but of power and of love and of a sound mind" (II Timothy 1:7).

To use your gifts for God, first rebuke the spirit of fear. Then claim the promise that God has given you a spirit of power, a spirit of love and a spirit of a sound mind. The result will be fruitful service to God and the expansion of

His Kingdom. The reward will be a resounding, "Well done, good and faithful servant. Enter into the joy of the Lord."

Let the anointing of God come upon you as you use your emotional personality to take more territory for the Kingdom of God! YOU CAN DO IT!!!

Ben R. Peters

*W*ith over 35 years of ministry experience, Ben Peters with his wife, Brenda, have been called to an international apostolic ministry of equipping and activating others. As founders and directors of Open Heart Ministries, Ben and Brenda have ministered to tens of thousands with teaching and prophetic ministry. The result is that many have been saved, healed and delivered and activated into powerful ministries of their own.

Ben has been given significant insights for the body of Christ and has written eight books in the past five years, since beginning a full-time itinerant ministry. His passions and insights include unity in the body of Christ, accessing the glory of God, five-fold team ministry and signs and wonders for the world-wide harvest.

The Peters not only minister at churches, camps, retreats and conferences, but also host numerous conferences with cutting-edge apostolic and prophetic leaders. They reside now in Northern Illinois with the youngest three of their five children, and travel extensively internationally.

Open Heart Ministries
www.ohmint.org
benrpeters@juno.com
15648 Bombay Blvd.
S. Beloit, IL 61080

Printed in the United States
127757LV00002B/1/A